THE BOOK OF WOMEN'S MYSTERIES
AND ONE MAN'S CONFUSION

 **Right Heart Press 2014**

Hope You like
the poems!

Feb 17/2015

nin

Ronald Kurt

Edmonton poet Ronald Kurt has published in over 30 literary magazines, including *The Antigonish Review*, *The Nashwaak Review*, *Prairie Fire* and *Toronto Life*. Poems have recently been published in the *Barrio Poster Series*. He is also the author of eight poetry chapbooks.

Some of these poems were previously published in the following publications:

"ROSE FOR A WOMAN"-- *Barrio Poetry Poster#77*
"THE POET'S BARE SOLES"-- *Barrio Poetry Poster#75*
"OVER HER CITY GARDEN"-- *Closing The Book On Darkness*
                              Chapbook (Reference West) 1996.
"SHAKESPEARE AFTERNOON"-- *The Canadian Forum*
                              September, 1978.
 "DREAMS OF A SOULMATE"-- 2013 Ascent Aspirations Publishing
                              Anthology.

TURNING A PAGE SLOWLY

Thankful for her grace
throughout the day.
The sacred silence when
I know my voice would
shatter the moment—
the necessary silence between
a man and a woman.
My voice would only dent
the magic. I fidget in my
mind for a sound to break
the spell. The spell only
a woman can conjure.
A shrug of her shoulder
or the narrowing of her
eyes glancing towards me.
There is respect and
consideration when she
finally speaks in a level
tone addressing the topic
at hand. Spiritual health,
physical health. The commitment
of the heart. Is the heart of a
man wild? Is a man's heart wary
of confinement? The voice of a
man afraid of crossing any line
is gentle, even shy.
A real man wants to love and
be loved. He wants to be mystified
by a woman's charms.
This is the pure circle from birth
to death. A man and a woman read
one and other like a holy book
always turning a page slowly
and carefully.

ROSE FOR A WOMAN

Step by step towards the red rose.
A careful yet hurried approach to
the first red rose of summer.
A woman is excited. There is a
sense of anticipation in her dreams.
A lover and a rose for a woman
long overdue, accepting with open
eyes this man's embrace before
allowing him to place red roses
in a bedside vase.

THE POET'S BARE SOLES

I saw the poet's bare soles.
They were pure white.
The bottoms of her toes
and the bottoms of her heels
were a light black. She had
been working in her garden
all day. Fellow poets and writers
of song listened to her while
she read to them standing
next to her freshly planted garden.
They took in the sounds and meanings
of her words as she stood barefooted
without sandals on sacred ground.

OVER HER CITY GARDEN

A small plot of earth
is a woman's Eden.

Blue flowers, fresh tomatoes.
Sea shell decorations around
certain plants. A crab apple
tree.

Secret songs spread their sounds
over her city garden racing
to the sky.

Her being embraces this vision
of perfection even with the wild
weed creeping for a place in paradise.

SHAKESPEARE AFTERNOON

A gentle press of my hand against your
breast as we sit in the basement.
You recite Shakespeare for your up-
coming audition, and I try to motivate
you.

You begin to weep, and I can't understand
if you are crying for the passages you
are reading, or if your heart and soul
are a vision of our happiness naked on the
couch.

DREAMS OF A SOULMATE

My neighbor calls frequently.
She's always in need of sugar,
bread or toilet paper.
Having known her for years
it's hard to say no or to ignore
her requests. It would appear
that the men in her life are available
for sex while she dreams of a soul
mate to take her away from alcohol
and cigarettes staining her morning
bed. God has a place in her life
when she prays for a lottery win.
Her barefoot walk and companionship
on cold winter nights, where we share
the body heat while looking for some
kind of enlightenment.

CLOSE WOUNDS

Poetry can save the poet
while the world tortures
the poet's soul.

Reading. Writing.
Words can close
wounds.

People are usually
the source of grief
diminishing the light.

A good poem
resurrects the body.

A full cup of gratitude
is raised to the true God.

A river of words
flows to and from
the poet's heart.

A DREAM FOR DREAMERS

Life should always be
fine food before you.
A perfect drink by
your hand and classical
music playing in the back-
ground. The weather should
be suited to your mood.
Wind, snow or rain.
Sunshine to awaken
a deep sleep. A disease-
free existence in a country
that is not plagued by religious turmoil.
This is how life should be.
It could always be a dream
for dreamers –
a stroke of luck in a broken world
waiting for oceans of love
to pour the wounds away.

Rusti L Lehay

Rusti L Lehay, an Edmonton poet and professional writer, has had poems appear in *On Spec*, *The Prairie Journal of Canadian Literature*, *FreeFall*, *Other Voices*, and on a spoken word collection with *Tupperware Sandpiper*. She once experienced a poet's dream when commissioned to write a poem for a Holland advertising agency. The poem then circulated in 4 European countries. Her limited edition chapbook *i'm not sure* (©1999) sold out.

One thing for sure, she is grateful for 16 years of poetry as audience and performer in the Stroll of Poets. And that the Stroll brought Anna Mioduchowska, Nancy Mackenzie, Julie Robinson, and Myrna Garanis into her life. Together with these fellow poets, *Eyeing the Magpie* was published in 2007.

So many blessings have come about through making several deep connections leading into great friendships with other poets. What more can a poet ask for?

"26 stingy gods" one version of it appeared in the 2006 Stroll of Poets
                    Anthology
"chasing scent of sky" appeared in Eyeing the Magpie
"beyond the frame" appeared in Eyeing the Magpie
"i have seen the wind" not published before
"wearing earth" not published before
"spontaneous combustion" not published before
"contrast" not published before
"watched moon never moves" not published before

26 stingy gods

ask you to lift a pen to page
you argue against extreme sports

like i'm asking you to climb everest
assigning you laborious tasks
find perfect handmade parchment
turn katmandu's tip upside down
dip its peak in indian's ocean of ink
now guide the granite nib
etch a gentle creative script

divining on the tip of your tongue
a stern-checked avalanche
i approach you sideways
seat you atremble at a keyboard
you claim twenty-six unruly gods
seven minions of punctuation confound you
refuse to arrange in visible thought

blunt points of your fingers
seal up silent conduits
your body a stiff atheistic prayer
muffled in quiet quicksand

but your hand melds into wooden spoon
and you stir verbal notions into pasta
your private wit deep and wild
slides out on steam
graces me a rare glimpse
your shy and reclusive imp of a muse
delivers thoughts on conditions
i never curl them into
flat black on white

chasing scent of sky

will i feel sliced open
when we fly through a rainbow
or is it our wings that split
noah's spectrum of colours

will i gaze upon your hands
caressing the stick
your eyes torn between
instrument panel and a violet strand arcing
neighbour to red orange yellow and green
beckoning our own bermuda triangle

will i hear the rainbow cry out
a blessing on the flying machine
we built with our own hands
whisper of cloud silk
tickling my freedom drenched ears

will i wear holy light for an eternity
my skin baptized by sun's gold dust
offer my body for your tongue to taste

will i trust gravity to suspend its laws
ask you to execute a dead stall
allowing me to twist my tongue
sampling ribbons of refracted light
taste sweet spiced jellied strips
dancing across taste buds

for this i'll trade my childhood dream
to split rain in halves around my flesh
small payment to forgo a lifelong urge
to stretch forth one hand into sun
bathe the other in rain

can you even begin to imagine
riding the scent of such joy

wearing earth

i've donned the full range of fluorescence
now home to prairie colors
forest greens catch my eye
saskatchewan skies of blue adorn my body
writing on stone earth colors for decoration
turquoise my favorite gem

spontaneous combustion

strike no matches
i am tinder dry
whole house could flame
my skin the dangerous accelerant

crisp and brittle inside out
skim my face   my palms
carpet burn bare skin
dirty thirty prairie cracks
adorn my fingertips

veins parch
dry bladder shrinks
rustle inside deafens me
grey matter likens to old concrete
risk of crumbling

wetter water isn't moist enough
four litres a day
fails to control this inner fire

beyond the frame

"A young woman on the shore" Paul Fischer

    i must glimpse what she strains to see
perched on a sandy sparse beach grass dune

    she wears a long soft cotton-cloud dress
belted by a black sash
    sea breezes
billow her wide skirt
    right hand firmly clutches
a straw hat's front brim
trimmed with a sable band

    crinkled up to the elbow
tight full length sleeves
reluctantly bare her sun-shy wrists
    her left hand dangles   obscured
red gingham swatch of cloth
towel   swimsuit   blanket   perhaps

    her face weaves deep desire
        does she spot a whale in mid breach
a ship of goods at port or yearn for a sailor beau
    maybe for sky pirates to come steal her away

before i casually wish for her side of the fence
i need some questions answered

    what lies behind her
her dress too crisp
for a dirt floor cabin
too white from hem to collar lace
    her shoulders stiff   her back straight
invisible books balanced on her crown
    i suspect her feet twice hidden
beneath the long hem behind sandy reeds
    lack calluses if bare
my only preview   this tableau
i cannot trade spots

her mansion born
    hidden chains are not for me
  but if it's a playful pod of whales spyhopping
pelicans in flight   a harbour full of sea-breeze choices
  just one big step outside that frame
    no past of my own to tug me back

    you'll know where i've gone

i have seen the wind

she expands her lungs
fills four dimensions
from aerobic floor to steel beam ceiling
legs to span equators
stretches her wall to wall
lithe body centered on a blue sponge mat

she knows no bounds
hovers above soiled trodden carpet
keeps her unprotected
white-clothed socked feet fresh as snow

beside her
an astrological day timer
her personal new millennium star chart
with the smallest of exhalations
she breezes through pages
one during each stretch
this wind can multi-task
chalky cumulus cloud shoes
patiently wait for her to gust

the loudspeaker blares her theme song
stairway to heaven but
everyone's oblivious
i pretend to lift my weights

entranced i watch this wind
staff's voice breaks through
attention sunshine spa members
solia to the front desk
she races off afloat
mid-air she slips
neat frosted feet
easily in shoes eager for flight
a desperate wind
keen to catch her astral travel agent
offering her bargain rates on heaven's tours
perfect for her sunny days off
zip back in time for next week's storm

at least that's what i
imagine as my eyes water
in the wake of her perfume

what happens if i am caught
spying on the wind

contrast

two women lust for flight
cast in shadow by their right breasts
both their men plummet into shining armour
sue dies when my hair trusts follicles
armour tarnished from overuse

your trust in life wanes
i still breathe
chuck falls down
black rabbit hole
twists and turns
his sue dead
reason to frown and wail
gnash his teeth on god's feet

and you
i wanted chuck to slap you silly
easier to just leave and live
i will not stand around
watching you count my breaths

watched moon never moves

but you'll move it
by telekinesis you say
for your perfectly composed picture
and drive the tides crazy
there'll be floods
and weather experts
will scratch
their collective heads
punch buttons and equations into
computers
and ask each other
el nino
no just some guy with a camera

Barbara Mitchell

Barbara Mitchell is an internationally award winning published poet, poetry judge, and producer of multi-media poetry/photo presentations.
She facilitates a variety of poetry/writing workshops,guiding and inspiring participants to reach new creative heights. "Never the Pretty One", included in this anthology, was published in *Room* literary magazine.

Barbara is also an accomplished mixed media artist who engages colour, collage and translucent glazes to her acrylic and encaustic works to create abstract visions out of the everyday. Her paintings have been showcased in many exhibitions and art shows. Her creations can be viewed at www.dancinginapotofpaint.com and at www.poetrycafe.ca.

water girl

the water girl waits for movement
a sign she is wanted –
she carries a flute tucked
in the gathering of her dress
a gold chain floats on her wrist
and all your secrets are balanced in her pocket

if you call to her she will come
the sweet note of metal will thrum her lips
while her hand curls into the silver –
this is the way she will curl into you
if you breathe her name into the rough patch
of your day

she is servant to your passion
she will find you behind the high court wall
bind your hands to the pavilion column

the water girl knows the way
to seduce you into stillness
the monologue of her attention
will soften the harsh lines of your life
her mouth, gentle out the laying down of your eyes
and later when you sleep
you dream of waterwheels
the caress of a wet cloth
hours soaked in rain

make me believe

make me believe
there is one last dance
that love is out there waiting
that passion still stirs beneath
this obstinate heart
that the resonance of spring might dance
through these weary limbs
that the lethargic spirit which binds me
might be lifted

let me believe there is one last dance
to shake loose my pale beliefs
my frail desires
where every dream I had has atrophied
unlock the stammering speech
the one i keep to myself
hidden in the back of my throat
stretch my tongue
that it might sing again
let my eyes ripen to the sights around me
let me believe
there is one last sunset
so brilliant
i will go down into death
with it blazing through the center of me
my veins glowing like silver threads
my whole body throwing off light
saying, yes, i have loved

i am the bird

i am the bird in the story
sitting silent on the sparse tree branch

i see the accident on the corner
the way the chrome indentation of someone's mistake
becomes someone else's blame
the way heat in voice rises
from the charged energy of collision
and i learn to say accident
or two people
or the word collision
and not swoop to redefine it
and i stay the silent bird in the story
i keep my own energy sparse
avoiding collision
so as not to absorb the blame
of someone else's mistake

i am the bird in the story
tamping down my voice
so as not to sing brilliantly
and lure their attention upward
away from the confrontation below

i am the story in the bird
rewriting its ending so as not to begin dancing
not to shake the leaves free from the tree
so that the color lights up the air
between collision and blame

i am the bird in the story
and i keep my countenance calm
so as not to swoop down on the accident
on the corner
i am the story rewriting the bird
as it rewrites the tree
as it learns to say accident
learns to just sit in the tree
learns to say
two cars or two people
or the word collision
and not swoop to redefine it–

i stay silent
i am the bird in the tree

direction

if the wind blows in a different direction
than what you are used to
feel it on your face
hear its whisper
but know that you do not have to follow it
and if the sun breaks through your eyes
and causes you to see something that hurts
that is too sharp for your vision
that is too ripe or not right for your line of thought
then shutter down
and be still
let the quiet invade your eyelid
let it sink you into its mercy and keep you safe
and if you are walking
and the moon illuminates the path
but it is a path that would lead you away
from what you know to be true of you
then move into the shadow
sit softly in the night's undercurrent
and let it breathe itself into you

fire dance

we dance in our primal goodness
and the wash of flame ignites our spirit
we feel the call of the wild
the pull of the untamed
and we are homing to our soul skin
it is our place of birth
the one that lives inside us
that internal flare we leave over and over
to enter the world
the one we are beckoned to
lured into
but when we come into our calm
and seek deliverance from chaos
we hold out our hands
throw them to the skies
and the fire pulls us in
and every sweet light danced off the flame
enters through the portal of our eye
flies to the heart
and all the days missed in-between
are but a vapor

always there

i am calling you across a distance
voice meshed like a soft wind
i am blowing softly past hours and time zones
can you hear me?

let the idle evening wrap itself around you
let it lull you into sleep
and if the breeze shifts in the bed you lie upon
know that it is me

i am favoring you in your darkness
inventing a dream only you can see
and in the pools of your resting eyes
i have seen myself balanced knee deep
somewhere between the past and the present
like the east and west wind inspiring communion
the kind that breaches the miles

i am calling you
can you hear me?
that persistent blur of scented motion
like the soft breath rising and falling
the small song
the one that warms you when you least expect it
you can never hold it
but it is always there

that sound you hear
it is me
calling your name over and over
down the hall of your sleep
can you hear me?

longest poem

you are my longest poem
the long slow
gentle one that goes on forever
the one written in the small hours
when the heart meets up with something so big
it doesn't know how to take it in
so it falls down and weeps
because it does not understand it...
that is when the poem that is you
writes itself closer
explaining things
to make the big things
seem less big
it is like all your beautiful words
heal the broken things in my life...
the sequence that is you in my day and hours
takes me
and rearranges me
so we fit into the long sentence
we are writing
you are my wordsmith
and together we weave
ourselves
into an undying language

never the pretty one

she dreams of white birds inhabiting her body
their plump forms pushing beneath
the mantle of collarbone
pressing up past sloped shoulders into proud posture
she imagines the cobra
uncoiling itself from sleep in the slouched
cave of her spine
stretching her to a lean line

she has had enough
of eyes shutting down when she walks by
blinking her to a vague impression
furtive glances skipping past her stories
she fears dying in a sluggish life
limping past adventure

she longs to waken in someone else's dream
fluid limbs dancing beneath a wafer of moon
she is keeper of dark mysteries
inflamed secrets
and she prowls the night
in search of sacred rhythms

she has had enough of speech that fails her
the oppressed silence
that shudders upward
from stifled bones

she longs for voice saturated in fluency
the anointing of rhyme
easy movement of word on word
she wants to steal into life like an explosion of verse
like a heart's fist turned inward
like a language doubled over
in grief
or laughter

tonight
she dreams she is woman reborn
a galaxy of beauty pivoting on an axis of grace
she is stunning stars into meteor showers
all eyes turn towards her
and the whole world spins on her image

Sandra Mooney-Ellerbeck

Sandra Mooney-Ellerbeck is an internationally published poet. "Imprints", the poem that continues to inspire, won tickets to Maya Angelou's talk at the Winspear in 2012 and was published in the Edmonton Journal. "Imprints" inspired an art and poetry collaboration showcased during StArts Fest 2013 – Sandra invites you to be inspired by "Imprints" in this anthology.

"Imprints", "Dramas", "Escape", and "Signs" are also included in Sandra's full length poetry collection, *Overlapping*, to be published soon. "Signs" was published in the award winning literary publication: CV2. "Another Year of Thirst" was published by *Barrio Art Posters*, distributed nationally to libraries, bookstores, and cafes. "In and Out of Sync" and "Word Combos" are new poems.

Sandra's poetic passion is in haiku -- haiku can be viewed at www.thehaikufoundation.org/resources/poet-details/?IDclient=219

Sandra is delighted to be part of another writing adventure with Right Heart Press and artist Izabela Ciechanowska.
Gratitude for:
What Can Be Held Onto - limited edition chapbook sold out in 2012.
Navigating Chaos with Ron Kurt and ky perraun - 2011
Bliss broadsheet - 2010

In and Out of Sync

Struggling to stay
between
Aegean waves
in calm retreat

beach sand, a dream
between
my toes squished in shoes –

my body rebels, thrust
back into routine-rush
each step on city sidewalk,
a side-ache in inner rhythm –

an elderly woman pauses
blocks conscious-time
gazes upward

what she sees
is beyond
my quickened pace –

the sun, a rest
relaxes my step,
argues against my pace
between
day-timer lines.

Escape

Grandmother grows fairies in her garden
poppy-wings flutter as I pause
to sprinkle seeds from pods and daydreams.

Summer wind shakes rose bushes –
I dance barefoot on fallen bouquets,
ask Dolia, fairy of fate
for magic words to release mother –

father can't rescue her, his long slow steps,
heavy as her depression, press
into the institution's manicured grass

when we visit

glass and brick imprison her wave
expressionless as her face
in the third story window.

Grandmother's garden is river air,
hummingbirds and butterflies,
winged-song and green scent
rooted in wonder deeper
than weeds.

Dramas

Mother is an Elizabeth Taylor look-alike –
her beauty is home-movie
immortalized
in wedding day white-lace,
in water-skis on Lake Okanagan –

even in the scene
where she lets go of swing-chains,
jumps, lands off balance, falls,
rises lake-soaked.

She walks the red carpet,
a celebrity of wellness
when she models
leather vests and skirts
at her sales clerk job
in the Bay's Leather Loft, and
when she walks the runway
holding serving trays at PTA teas.

Every five years
she changes like gray tones between
black-and-white, between
sickness-and-wellness –

her moments become ashes
in the bottom of an ashtray,
smoked away like her thoughts –

we watch

a molotov cocktail
of chemical imbalance
explode like Elizabeth Taylor's
emotional cinema dramas
ending with credits
followed by blank screens.

Mother always comes back altered
after two month's hospitalization:
    less depressive
    or less manic –
her true self, always known by her arms
reaching out, always reaching out –
her love never needs resuscitation
like her mind.

Word Combos

fogged in Frisco, a new generation
yick yacks, yack yicks
around round bistro tables at the Vesuvio –
small talk, heads up, down, down, up, texting –

voices levitate above bar and TV screen
first floor to second –
mingle in
chit chat, chat chit
gossip –

i fold hands in reverence above Kerouac
on white and black art deco table top,
flesh on icon –
poetic lines, his/mine
mingle in
sips of red wine, vintage wine,
vintage words –

ghost rhythms on the beat of memory
frolic in stale air above stilettos on tile
click, clack, clack, click

click clack, clack click
yick yack, yack yick
chit chat, chat chit
empty of poetness bliss

Another Year of Thirst

I call on ancestors of this parched prairie,
put on feathers and turquoise,
body paint and bracelets –
moccasin men and barefoot women
mask together in zigzag dance,
tap the dust in rhythmic patterns.

I call on river spirits to divine
the sandbars—draw
water from the depths—
flood cracking banks.

I call on believers in answered prayer,
raise hands to the cloudless sky,
pour praises into the wind, conjure
more than mirage storms—

even the forest is dehydrated
under rotting deadfall—
moss is an un-wetted sponge
fraying—

sprouts of spruce are burnt orange,
each needle is no more than an idea
falling.

I dip a bucket into the rain barrel,
scoop out last October's rain,
offer parched roots a drink—
April wind sucks my deed—

chickadees smell the drying dirt,
fly to me as if anticipating winter seed—
call on me as if my hands are spring rain.

Imprints

Remember, as pine cones remember
when to be evergreen, as deciduous trees
remember when to bud, to leaf,
to let go and sleep dream. Remember,
as migratory birds remember when to unfurl
and when to fold their wings,
as the sun knows dawn and dusk,
as the moon knows all cycles. Remember,
as lakes remember when to be ice,
when to be in wave, and when to be still,
as each sea knows each river and each river
knows the rain and melted snow,
as soil knows each seed, and each seed knows
what to become and when to give more seed.
Remember, as mountains remember
each fossil, crevasse, and cliff,
as each underground layer knows its purpose,
as jungles know they are not deserts, as deserts
know they will always thirst. Remember,
as the sky remembers how to coexist with you,
as new life cries a first breath, as a heart beats
in time to your rhythm –
and, when your air is the last breath I breathe,
remember what I became and gave
because of being –
remember as you remember
your orbit.

Signs

The artificial red rose is our lasting connection—
we talked about it like the weather ever since
she told me afterlife stories, the signs, seemingly
supernatural, that convinced her, led her
to make a pact with grandfather,
that led to the pact I made with her, with the rose,
the rose in the crystal vase that has been on my
bedroom dresser for twenty-five years, the rose
that hasn't changed since my husband gave it to me
after I asked him to stop
giving me roses that die.

While her breathing labored death, the last sentence
I said to her was: Remember the rose.

I thought she would take the rose out of the vase and
lay it down, or move the vase to another place like she
thought grandfather's spirit
moved her soup bowl across their kitchen table.

On the third morning after her last breath,
one of the rose petals bent outward,
separated from the rest.

ky perraun

ky perraun has been published in various literary journals, including *The Prairie Journal*, *Jones Av* and *Notebook*; and anthologies, including *Standing Together*, *Navigating Chaos*, *As One Cradles Pain*, *In New Light*, and *40 Below*. She performs her poems with her partner, the musician Vicktor Pannewitz.

"Hazards of the Art" was published in *The Prairie Journal of Canadian Literature*

"Renewed Life" is in the anthology *Standing Together*

"The Atmosphere" and "The Distance of Time" are in the chapbook *Prayers and Graffiti* (Greensleeves Publishing, 1990)

HAZARDS OF THE ART
(for Ronald Kurt)

What I was eager to know about poets
was whether they got depressed.
Your eyes widened, as though I had asked
something relevant, but close to the bone.
You said they did. I felt less alone.

You then introduced me to free verse
and a host of poets, all of whom,
I assumed, sang the blues from honest places,
yourself included.

Later, when I went mad, it seemed
a hazard of the art, perhaps a pedigree.

Thirty one years have gone by, and I still turn
to you for affirmation of this cursed gift
with which we wrestle.

With our prescriptions and meagre possessions,
our pens and pain, we belong to a breed
destined to live on the edge, to leave a legacy
of lines culled from the depths of despair,
archaeologists of the psyche, predicting disaster,
while tasting the sweet fruit of the bending branch
upon which we perch.

PRAIRIE LAKE

These are sacred waters to the descendants
of French and Cree – weed-green and soft,
risen to the retaining wall, having swallowed
the beach. I have no belief, only memories
of first blood and promenades down dirt roads,
past the lust-filled eyes of boys with their wet
dreams and confusion, and the water's cool
caress on hot afternoons.

I am in my fifth decade now, full of the debris
of middle aged thought, mounds of concepts
that block the light. Though I try to enter
the water as a pilgrim, I emerge a tourist,
checking off stars in an internet review –

murky depths, ankle-grabbing fronds, small,
toe-stubbing rocks, crowds and exhaust
from Main Street. Forgive me, father, but this
shrine is second-rate, and the only miracle
is the minnows I didn't swallow when I dunked
my head in a mock baptism, and my vision
was of the hamburger stand where ice cream cones
were being built by teenage workers, to whom
I bequeath the magic of a prairie lake in July.

THE ATMOSPHERE

What is that stillborn star, tucked
in the sky – luminescent shiver
of moon, my slate-bearded Norse god
lumbering his way through the caves.

And what are we, if not tragedy
served up on the king's dinner plate,
slit-throat sacrifices separate
from the still-ripened breast. It's best
that we speak of these things, if only
to frighten our hearts.

Although the trees lay crippled, and old
homes eaten by marketplace teeth, this immediate
release of damp heat feels lovely, like the holy
apex coming home
against the rage of July.

I've hung the sterilized cotton
out on the harbour to dry. Many nights
baptized, many nights gone, and nothing
but these beckoning frames
click through the rain
a sutured virginity
a damp acceptance of fate.

And yet, we create our own destinies –
ultimate freedom in that! With every crack
of each branch, God dies with the rabbits
and rats.

'Hold me,' you said, 'like a lifeboat –
there's more where this fever came from.
I am drenched, and feeling diseased.'

We, so timid of our imperfections,
having walked through the blind velvet rope,
we believe in eternity, bow
in the face of one day.

If the calendar was rearranged
this whole scene would change
no rain would ruin hard-won words
no envy would mock from the stage.

Age. You call it unfolding.
I call it a curse, and worse:
No prayer can smudge it away.

Only rain falls. No mountains quiver.
Mustard seeds in the heat. Defeat
crawls up beside me, dances its passion
through my thigh.

The sky closes in, sparking vacancies,
ten thousand ends to the night, while
light, the fickle redeemer, retreats
to the safety of heat.

Have you no pity, my planet?
Have you no feel for disguise?
Or is it I, amongst constant confusion
imagining love's ride in the hearse?

RENEWED LIFE

My lover returns from the world with a bouquet
and meal. He reads my poem
with a red pencil, shaves the odd word
but preserves most lines.

After dinner he composes music
and I swallow my medicine.

The wooden desk, the pale chrysanthemums
the beautiful concoctions that steady the mind.
His skin, my heart, this life
like a phoenix flying into the future
with no room for remorse.

All phantoms banished to books
our bed strewn with new memories
of tenderness, lucidity and love.

POOR RHUBARB

The rhubarb spreads its grey-green fan
to shade the life burrowing amongst its roots,
its fruit sour and sinewy, inedible, really,
without heat and sugar, but blood tonic,
nonetheless.

I admire its hardiness in this northern clime,
imagine deep dish pies and jam, sugary clouds of steam
rising from a bubbling pot.

Prehistoric, its form, its stems stale-blood red.
Reaching out to pale pink roses, it resembles
a rich, homely man wooing a young virgin
with trips and diamonds, incongruous with appearance.

I smile and let the flirtation proceed,
knowing the rose prefers the impoverished acrobat,
the petunia, whom it will marry in a nosegay
upon a table, where poor rhubarb will float
in a puddle of cream, flaky crust a devised disguise,
and fill our bellies with thick, softened stalks.

THE DISTANCE OF TIME
(for music)

Ah, my love, I sent to you
my memories tied in a veil.
Ah, my love, I crawled to you
my energies sentenced to fail.
Ah, my love, my solitude,
my prophecy could not foresee
how my love enraptured me
my ecstasy burning in,
burning in me.

I waved to you as the sky broke free. I
waved to you as you said we were not
meant to be apart like this, and I knew
the bright memory of our last kiss
burned much stronger
in the distance of time.

Our love was a mirror, our love
was a lake, freezing and reflective –
I could not partake. We gazed together
and we played a part on a stage
which nobody owned.

I wrote to you that I'd always be true.
You replied with my solitude. And so,
alone, we paced those islands
and no one touched us but ourselves.

Ah, my love, I lent to you
ceremonies bloody and dull.

Ah, my love, I bought for you
your tragedies, the heroine culled.
Ah, my love, my servitude
my discipline could not grant me
the right to claim so easily
that which you had promised me
should I heed your silent plea.
Please, set me free.

CYPRESS HILLS, 5 a.m.
(for Vic)

"Poetry, too, seeks a place in the world –
feasting on darkness but needing light,
taking confession, listening for bells,
for the first strains of music in town square."
-Edward Hirsch
"Krakow, Six A.M."

The mist-limp page absorbs the pen's issue,
pigment feathering into softened plumes,
as on a Japanese rice paper scroll,
the poet's loneliness evident in calligraphy's curves,
her pure, poignant isolation, scribbling missives in half-light,
fuelled by the desire for immortality, her legacy
a small slice of wisdom, portioned from the vast expanse
of her observed universe, her ache for a listener,
some eyes, tired or new, to read and absorb
as the page now drinks the ink and rain,
the sweat and tears
of the only conscious resident
amongst this city of sleepers.

USED BOOK
(for Roo Borson)

Poetry. Canadian. $10. – pencilled on the fly-leaf.
And from this sale the poet will not prosper. But the price
is right, and what are we in this for anyhow, it can't be
the money, not here, in this vast land of spaces and trucks,
its underfunding and penchant for the alienating obscure.

This once-loved book will be devoured, I assure you,
like a croissant in a complimentary breakfast in a hotel
on the prairies after a night of bad coffee and bedbugs –
relished, in short. It will spur my imagination on to new
heights, and spend the remainder of its days on a cedar
shelf, where it will assume some of the perfume and all
of the grandeur of that tree. (Paper is to wood as morphine
is to heroin.)

Thank you for writing, for believing in words when industry
conspired to mould you into an uber-consumer and the glossies
pedalled paradise in a prefab kitchen. Thank you for working
your fingers to the bone on similes that surprise, and for
the unspoken bond between metaphor and the machinery
of the mind, all without the promise of material independence,
or your photo in the tabloids. Let me be your paparazzi via
poetry, record your near-naked images as they frolic at the public
pool, exploit your assonance as it wiggles away in a working
class pub, with CMT on the screen and draft glasses writing
O, O, O on Formica. Let me repay you for the hours of enlightenment,
the long drive into the mind of a woman who sees without filters
the mysteries.

I have no money.

Dani Zyp

Dani began to write stories at a tender age. This is her second anthology and she self-published three of her own books. Supported by family and friends she continues to publish, participate in readings and write new words. Young at heart, she recently further developed this soul-work by composing original songs.

She teaches work shops in self-publishing.

Eagle's Flight

One day, as she sat comfortable
On the deck of Lusty Heights –
The sun warming her skin
The peace and quiet warming her soul
She felt the feathered touch
Of the Eagle's wing

Her spirit rose
Her heart beat strong
The leaves on the trees rustled with delight
As they flew up and up

Once above the earth
She could see everything
All through the eyes of the Eagle
They swooped and soared
The lakes, the mountains, the sky all around them
She came to know the Eagle's wisdom

All living things
Are imbued with powers super-natural
Birds and beasts in harmony
Humanity and earth in harmony

The sun warms the earth
The sea reflects the stars

Down below she saw the people
Grieving, crying, wailing in pain
And in a great surge
She felt the strength of love and community
The people began to sing, dance, laugh
Working together
And she felt the joy of the unification of life
Everlasting love

She opened her eyes to the stillness and dark
She was back down to earth
Through soaring Eagle's flight
she had reached Lusty Heights.

Liberate the Children

liberate the children
above and below
the 49th parallel

betwixt and between
from latitude 53 and beyond

we ask for universal public
healing centres
health care for everyone

today
to honour world poetry day
world water day
clean air day
arbour day

today
we say a prayer
we sing a song
we meditate
we chant to the beat
of the drum

access to quality of life
health care
is a human right
for everyone

change and transformation
are necessary to
our collective growth

change for the
better
change for the
child

.

Mission Possible

Seeking to go
Beyond equality
To justice –
For women
And men
African people
Afghani people
Mexicans, Iranians, Iraqis
Canadians…

World-wide justice:
An underground swell
Encouraging better
Food distribution
Organic farms
Sustainable livelihoods

Clean free water
Unpolluted air
Guaranteed Annual Income
Give each person what they need
To go beyond survival to thrive

Work to help our humanity
Our depth of love
Our collective health
Abundance for body, mind and spirit
Wholistic health

Universal Love Is...

Standing together
While I was
Standing alone

Knowing how it is
To be apart
Torn apart

Tears dripping like
The cover on this book
Engraved in one
Side of my face

I've learned much
Good, not bad
Not enough, too much

Standing on my own
Like a man

It works for me
Left brain thinking
And walkin' with my whiskey

Right brain thinking
And playing my music
with brush and harp
straight from the heart

a woman's domain now

you don't see my beauty
you just want me to be
a typical at-your-service
woman

I have plans and dreams and
Traditions of my own

I have love within my soul

I am no longer traumatized
By you, and you, and you
Pulling daggers from my heart

Healing the wounds of love

Love is universal…
Not chosen

It grows exponentially
Feeds on itself

And thus, I love you
Despite the pain
As a lover
As a friend
As a co-conspirator of this life
Time passages
Allowing us to breathe
Clear and free

Universal love is…
Not chosen

Yet given and received
With a full heart
An open soul
From self to self
Standing together
While standing alone

Universal love is…

People

Raped and pillaged
Broken bones of love
Cancer ravaged
Hallucinations of mental illness
Loss after loss after loss
Families and single mothers
Hungry – should they eat the mouse in the house?
Beaten up
Abused
Bed bugs
No heat
Frozen cold
Sleeping in a garage
A cardboard box
Under – the bridge
No identification
No job
No hope
Housing First
Gives the homeless a home
Sanctuary – heal time
Reflection on a full belly
A restful sleep
The passage of light and shadow
Balance and equilibrium
Regrouping
Recollecting the self
While home is wherever you find yourself
Creature comforts give the soul a container
A chance to focus beyond survival
And could save lives
In this harsh and unforgiving climate
Give a home with love

Stop Rape Now

There is no reason…(3x)

Not what she wears
Not what she does
Nor what she says
There is no reason…(3x)
Not yesterday
Not tomorrow
Not today
There is no reason…(3x)

Is there a way/ to get through to you/ it's not ok/ you can't get away/
(drum) you will pay/ you will hear the women rage…

Kinetic control/ kinetic control/
A marionette/ with strings attached/ you'll lose control/ of her soul/
you gave her pain/ and searing shame
No means no (3x)
Kinetic control/ kinetic control/
Under puppet control/ you took her soul/ a little death/ now we're bereft/
you took control/ though she said no
no means no (3x)

there is no reason…(3x)
against her will/ she wanted to kill
there is no reason…(3x)

STOP RAPE NOW! (drum) (repeat)

1 in 4 women and 1 in 8 boys are sexually abused by the time they are 18.
80% of assaults occur in the victim's home.
- 2014 Rape Support Network
  (Source: Justice Institute of British Columbia)

Women's Day

International Women's Day
Has sprung
Like spring in my heart
Asking for a love of Canada to return
A love from Canada as
A peacekeeping country

My mother
Mater
Mum
In the winter of her years
Looking fresh as tulips
Tight in the bud
Takes me there

I think of the babe
Lamb of god
Hugged in my arms
Cradled like a child
Bottle fed
Rejected by its mother
Well, she only had two teats
And triplet babes
(Can I keep a lamb in my downtown digs?)

Women. My favorite people
Let's celebrate our
Strength and diversity
Our walks on common ground
Our collaborative celebration
Of springing forth in the heart
The brain and the spirit
A holistic branching
Forth into
Preventive practices for all
Giving economic sense to health care
How love at every level
Can move us all forward
In the step of life

"It keeps coming at you"
my wise girlfriend warns
and my mom knows
you've got to watch out for
curve balls
like
a flower coming out of the earth
(Don't step on it!)
And monarch butterflies in Victoria

Far from Mexico where they are born
Mothers of butterflies
Surrounded by children
"A hungry child cannot learn"
women cry

Let us find peace this spring
All creatures of every creed, race and belief

Tulips *Eten*

grandmother spent a long time with

deer eating tulips off her grave

I gaze at the space
where she is not
through the long basement window
dappled light of the sun
making small inroads
for the deep...
deer scatter at the slightest
a welcome interruption
gentle motions
 heal, soothe psychic balms,
bonds of love to replace
shards from all the shrapnel

A peaceful time after the "move"
freshness of innocent children
always in her eyes
oma's m.o.
irresistible to opa
forever alive this love
 walks through eternity

tree boughs bowed together

every aspect

a different turn,
angles some and others angels of light
fresh-cut crystal
broken and repaired, broken and repaired
broken and repaired...unspoken for -
hear a soft-spoken voice
become loud?
A quiet note on high: "Enough!"
becomes louder
resonant
a cry high enough to shatter

Izabela Ciechanowska

Izabela Ciechanowska is a freelance illustrator living in Edmonton, Alberta. She has contributed illustrations to previous Right Heart Press publications and has also been published in Notebook magazine.

About the Cover:

"The Lark's Flight towards Truth" – ink on paper

The lark in mythology and literature is a symbol of daybreak and the messenger between heaven and earth. This piece represents the spiritual and physical escape and our exploration towards light and answers.

Made in the USA
Charleston, SC
17 January 2015